EXPLORE THE U.S.A.

NEVADA

Megan Kopp

LET'S READ
AV²
BY WEIGL™
ADDED VALUE • AUDIO VISUAL

Go to **www.av2books.com**, and enter this book's unique code.

BOOK CODE

Y610362

AV² by Weigl brings you media enhanced books that support active learning.

AV² provides enriched content that supplements and complements this book. Weigl's AV² books strive to create inspired learning and engage young minds in a total learning experience.

Your AV² Media Enhanced books come alive with...

Audio
Listen to sections of the book read aloud.

Video
Watch informative video clips.

Embedded Weblinks
Gain additional information for research.

Try This!
Complete activities and hands-on experiments.

Key Words
Study vocabulary, and complete a matching word activity.

Quizzes
Test your knowledge.

Slide Show
View images and captions, and prepare a presentation.

... and much, much more!

Published by AV² by Weigl
350 5th Avenue, 59th Floor
New York, NY 10118
Website: www.av2books.com   www.weigl.com

Library of Congress Cataloging-in-Publication Data
Kopp, Megan.
Nevada / Megan Kopp.
   p. cm. -- (Explore the U.S.A.)
Includes bibliographical references and index.
ISBN 978-1-61913-375-4 (hard cover : alk. paper)
F841.3.K67 2012
979.3--dc23
                    2012015091

Printed in the United States of America in North Mankato, Minnesota
1 2 3 4 5 6 7 8 9 16 15 14 13 12

052012
WEP040512

Project Coordinator: Karen Durrie
Art Director: Terry Paulhus

Weigl acknowledges Getty Images as the primary image supplier for this title.

NEVADA

Contents

3

This is Nevada.
It is called the Silver State.
Silver is found in Nevada.

5

6

This is the shape of Nevada. It is in the west part of the United States. Nevada borders five other states.

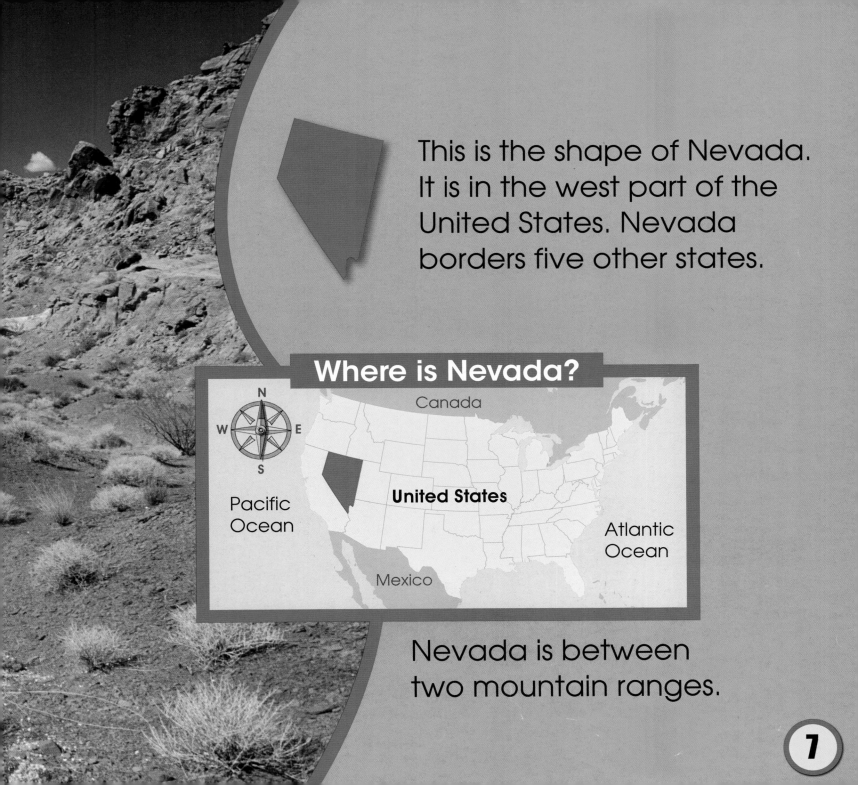

Where is Nevada?

Canada

N
W E
S

Pacific Ocean

United States

Atlantic Ocean

Mexico

Nevada is between two mountain ranges.

People hunted mammoths, bison, and reindeer in Nevada long ago. Hunters used tools made from stone.

Some ancient people lived in caves and made pictures on rock.

The sagebrush is the Nevada state flower. Its strong smell keeps animals from eating it.

The state seal has mountains, a train, and a mill.

One of the mountains has a tunnel.

THE GREAT SEAL OF THE STATE OF

ALL FOR OUR COUNTRY

NEVADA

This is the state flag of Nevada. It has a gold ribbon and sagebrush.

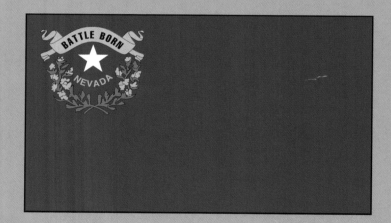

There is a white star on the flag.

The state animal of Nevada is the desert bighorn sheep. Bighorn sheep live in the mountains.

A desert bighorn sheep can go many days without drinking water.

This is Carson City. It is the Nevada state capital.

The largest amount of silver in the world was found near Carson City.

GOVERNOR'S
MANSION
→

17

Gold, silver, and copper are found in Nevada. There are about 20 gold mines in the state.

Nevada makes more than $4 billion each year from gold.

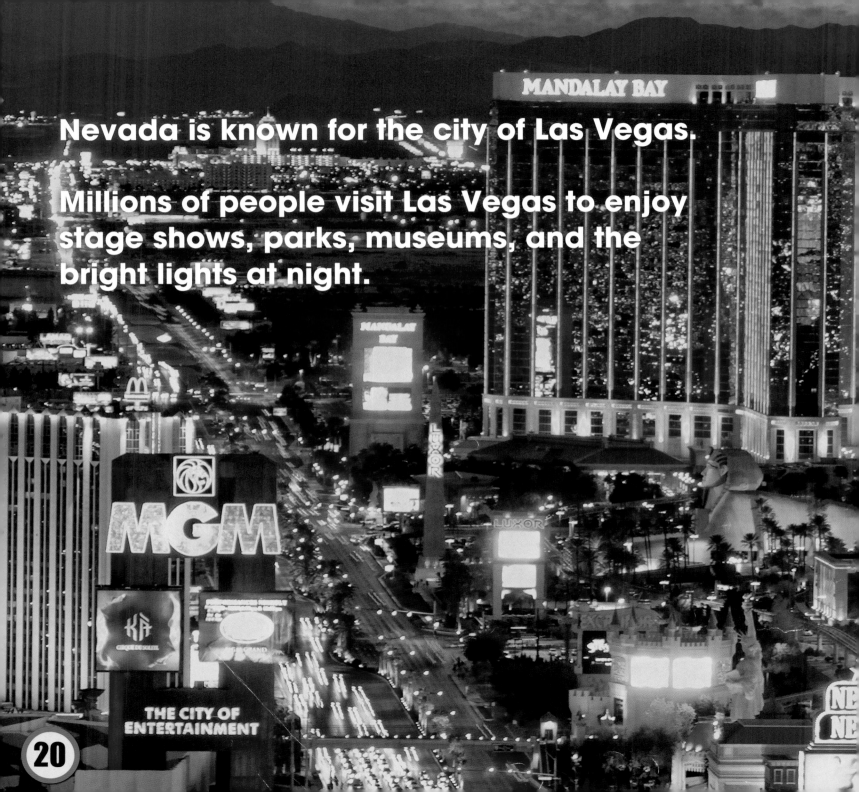

Nevada is known for the city of Las Vegas.

Millions of people visit Las Vegas to enjoy stage shows, parks, museums, and the bright lights at night.

NEVADA FACTS

These pages provide detailed information that expands on the interesting facts found in the book. These pages are intended to be used by adults as a learning support to help young readers round out their knowledge of each state in the *Explore the U.S.A.* series.

Pages 4–5

Nevada is called the Silver State because of its silver mines. The discovery of silver deposits called the Comstock Lode caused a silver rush in 1859. Virginia City was settled overnight and became "the richest place on Earth." The Coeur Rochester Mine opened in 1986. It is one of the largest silver mines in North America, producing 6 million ounces (170 million grams) of silver annually.

Pages 6–7

On October 31, 1864, Nevada became the 36th state to join the United States. The state lies on rugged highland between the Sierra Nevada and Rocky Mountain ranges in the western United States. Nevada is located almost entirely in the Great Basin region. It borders California, Oregon, Idaho, Utah, and Arizona.

Pages 8–9

Evidence of humans in Nevada dates back about 11,000 years. Prehistoric campsites have been discovered at Tule Springs. Stone and bone tools show people existed at the same time as later Ice Age mammals. Pictographs and petroglyphs have been found on rock overhangs and in caves in other parts of Nevada.

Pages 10–11

Sagebrush is Nevada's official state flower. It is a woody shrub that bears yellow flowers. The state seal has symbols for mining, transportation, communication, agriculture, and nature. The state motto, "All for our country," and 36 stars border the seal. The stars symbolize Nevada's place as the 36th state to join the Union.

The Nevada state flag has a blue background. The upper left corner has a star between two sprays of sagebrush. The ribbon above the sagebrush says "Battle Born," reflecting the state joining the Union side during the Civil War.

The desert bighorn sheep is found in the mountains of southern Nevada. The sheep can survive several days without drinking water. The plants they eat provide enough moisture for survival. There are about 13,000 desert bighorn sheep living in Nevada, California, Arizona, and Utah.

Carson City's name comes from the Carson River. Explorer John C. Frémont named the river for Kit Carson, a frontiersman and scout he hired for an expedition. In 1842, Carson and Frémont surveyed and mapped Nevada. The Comstock Lode silver strike was made near Carson City.

Nevada is one of the country's top mineral-producing states. The state leads the nation in gold production. Other mining products include barite, clay, mercury, and lithium. More than 12,000 people work in the mining industry in Nevada.

The city of Las Vegas is Nevada's most popular tourist destination. Millions of people visit the city each year. There are many hotels, museums, shows, and amusement parks in Las Vegas. The city is famous for its neon lights. More than 15,000 miles (24,140 kilometers) of neon tubing make the signs and symbols in Las Vegas glow.

KEY WORDS

Research has shown that as much as 65 percent of all written material published in English is made up of 300 words. These 300 words cannot be taught using pictures or learned by sounding them out. They must be recognized by sight. This book contains 54 common sight words to help young readers improve their reading fluency and comprehension. This book also teaches young readers several important content words, such as proper nouns. These words are paired with pictures to aid in learning and improve understanding.

Page	Sight Words First Appearance
4	found, in, is, it, state, the, this
7	between, mountain, of, other, part, two, where
8	and, from, lived, long, made, on, people, pictures, some, used
11	a, animals, has, its, keeps, one
12	there, white
15	can, days, go, many, water, without
16	near, was, world
19	about, are, each, makes, more, than, year
20	at, city, for, lights, night, to

Page	Content Words First Appearance
4	Nevada, silver
7	ranges, shape, United States
8	bison, caves, hunters, mammoths, reindeer, rock, stone, tools
11	flower, mill, sagebrush, seal, smell, train, tunnel
12	flag, ribbon, star
15	desert bighorn sheep
16	capital, Carson City
19	copper, gold, mines
20	Las Vegas, museums, parks, stage shows

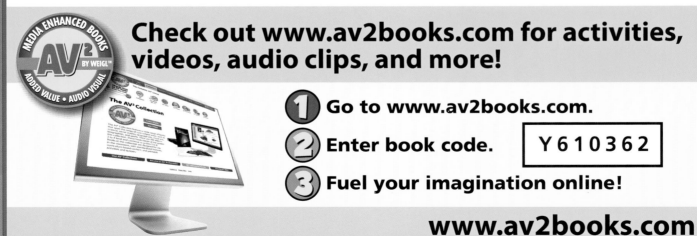